THE LIFE OF JOAN OF ARC

UUID: 12282590-e1d9-11e4-9580-1ba58673771c

This ebook was created with BackTypo (http://backtypo.com) by Simplicissimus Book Farm

Table of contents

CHAPTER I. THE CHILDHOOD OF JOAN OF ARC — 2

CHAPTER II. HOW THE VOICES CAME TO THE MAID — 9

CHAPTER III. HOW THE MAID OBEYED THE VOICES — 12

CHAPTER IV. HOW JOAN HEARD NEWS STRANGELY — 15

CHAPTER V. HOW THE MAID SAW THE DAUPHIN — 20

CHAPTER VI. HOW THE MAID RODE TO ORLEANS — 24

CHAPTER VII. HOW THE MAID SAVED ORLEANS — 28

CHAPTER VIII. HOW THE MAID TOOK THE TOWN OF JARGEAU — 33

CHAPTER IX. HOW JOAN DEFEATED THE ENGLISH IN FAIRFIELD — 36

CHAPTER X. HOW JOAN LED THE DAUPHIN TO BE CROWNED — 42

CHAPTER XI. HOW THE MAID WAS BETRAYED AT PARIS — 46

CHAPTER XII. HOW THE MAID TOOK CERTAIN TOWNS — 50

CHAPTER XIII. HOW THE VOICES PROPHESIED EVIL — 53

CHAPTER XIV. HOW THE MAID WAS TAKEN — 56

CHAPTER XV. THE CAPTIVITY OF THE MAID — 61

CHAPTER XVI. THE TRIAL OF THE MAID   65
CHAPTER XVII. HOW THE PRIESTS BETRAYED THE MAID   71
CHAPTER XVIII. THE END OF THE MAID   74
CHAPTER XIX. THE SECOND TRIAL OF THE MAID   77

CHAPTER I. THE CHILDHOOD OF JOAN OF ARC

JOAN OF ARC was perhaps the most wonderful person who ever lived in the world. The story of her life is so strange that we could scarcely believe it to be true, if all that happened to her had not been told by people in a court of law, and written down by her deadly enemies, while she was still alive. She was burned to death when she was only nineteen: she was not seventeen when she first led the armies of France to victory, and delivered her country from the English.

Joan was the daughter of a poor man, in a little country village. She had never learned to read, or write, or mount a horse. Yet she was so wise that many learned men could not puzzle her by questions: she was one of the best riders in France; one of the most skilled in aiming cannons, and so great a general that she defeated the English again and again, and her army was never beaten till her King deserted her. She was so brave that severe wounds could not stop her from leading on her soldiers, and so tender-hearted that she would comfort the wounded English on the field of battle, and protect them from cruelty. She was so good that her enemies could not find one true story to tell against her in the least thing; and she was so modest that in the height of her glory she was wishing to be at home in her father's cottage, sewing or spinning beside her mother.

Joan, who was born at Domremy, in the east of France, on January 6, 1412, lived in a very unhappy time. For nearly a hundred years the kings of England had been trying to make themselves kings of France, just as they had been trying to make themselves kings of Scotland. Perhaps they might have succeeded, if they had confined themselves to one conquest at a time. But they left Scotland alone while they were attacking France, and then Scotland sent armies to help the French, as at other times the French sent armies to help Scotland.

Eight years before Joan was born a sad thing happened to her country. Henry V. of England had married the Princess Katherine of France, and the French, or some of them, tired of being beaten in war, consented to let the child of Henry and the Princess Katherine be their King, instead of the son of their old King. The old King's son was called "the Dauphin"; that was the title of the eldest son of the French kings. This Dauphin was named Charles. His friends went on fighting the English for his sake, but he was not crowned King. The coronations of French Kings were always done in the Cathedral at Rheims, where they were anointed with sacred oil. The oil was kept in a very old flask, which was said to have been brought from heaven, to a Saint, by an Angel. No eldest sen of the King was thought really King of France, after his father's death, till he had been anointed with this heavenly oil at Rheims by the Archbishop. It is important to remember this; you will see the reason afterwards. Now, Rheims was in the power of the English, so the Dauphin, Charles, could not go there and be made King in earnest. The English said that he was not the son of his father, the late King, which made him very unhappy. We shall hear how Joan comforted him and made him King for good and all.

What Scots and Frenchmen could not do, she did.

In the meantime the French were divided into two parties. Some sided with the Dauphin, Prince Charles; more, and especially all the people of Burgundy, and the Duke of Burgundy, a great and rich country, were on the side of the English. So they fought very cruelly, for the land was full of companies of ill-paid soldiers, who plundered the poor, so that towns fell into decay, many fields were empty of sheep and cows, and the roads became covered with grass. In the villages a boy used to watch all day, from the spire of the church, to see whether any soldiers were riding up. If they came, the cattle were driven into the woods, and men, women, and children ran to hide themselves, carrying such things away as they could. The soldiers of all sorts robbed equally, for they had often no regular pay, and the Scots were not behindhand in helping themselves wherever they went. Even gentlemen and knights became chiefs of troops of robbers, so that, whoever won in the wars, the country people were always being plundered.

In the middle of these miseries Joan was born, in a village where almost everybody was on the side of the Dauphin: the right side. In the village nearest to hers, Maxey, the people took the English side, and the boys of the two places had pitched battles with sticks and stones. It is true that they would have found some other reason for fighting, even if the English had not been in France. Joan used to see her brothers, Peter and John, come home from these battles with their noses bleeding, and with black eyes, but she did not take part herself in these wars.

Her village was near a strong-walled town called Vaucouleurs, which was on the side of the Dauphin. When Joan was a little girl she did not see very much of the cruelty of the soldiers; the village was only visited once or twice by enemies. But she heard of what was going on in the rest of France: "there was great pity in France," she said. She did, once or twice, see some of the "pity." There was a man called Henry d'Orly, living in a castle named Doulevant, who, like many other gentlemen in these days, was a captain of robbers.

One day several spearmen of his rode into Domremy, Joan's village, and seized Joan's father's cows, with all the other cows that they could find, just as the Scotts, Elliots, and Armstrongs used to ride across the Border and drive the cattle of the English farmers. But a lady lived in a strong castle rear Domremy, and when she heard how the village people had been plundered she sent the news to a gentleman in the neighbourhood, who gathered his spearmen and rode after the robbers. The thieves, of course, could not ride faster than the stolen cows could trot; they pricked the poor beasts with their spears, and made them lumber along, but a cow is slow at best. The pursuers galloped and came on the cattle in a little town, while the thieves were drinking in the wine shops. When they heard the horses of the pursuers gallop down the street, they mounted their horses and spurred for their lives; but now came their master, Henry d'Orly, with more spearmen, who followed after the cattle and the gentlemen who were driving them home. They turned and charged Henry d'Orly, and cleared the road, and the cows came home to Domremy, all safe.

Another time all the people in Domremy had to fly from home, and go to a town called Neufchâteau, where they were safe behind strong walls. They only stayed there for a few days, but, later, the English said that Joan had been a servant in an inn at this town, and had learned to ride there, which was quite untrue.

Joan hanging garlands on the fairy oak

There were beautiful woods near the village, and in one oak wood an oak called the Fairy Tree. There was a story that a beautiful fairy used to meet her lover at that tree, just as under the Eildon Hill, the Queen of Fairyland met Thomas the Rhymer. The children used to take cakes, and make feasts, and hang garlands of flowers on the boughs of that oak; but Joan did not care much about fairies, and preferred to lay her wild flowers beneath the statues of Saints in the village Church, especially St. Catharine and St. Margaret. Of course, all this was long before the Reformation in which the Protestants broke the images of Saints in the churches, and smashed their pictures on the glass windows with stones, and destroyed a beautiful statue of Joan on the bridge at Orleans.

These things were done more than a hundred years after Joan was dead.

Though Joan could run faster than the other girls and boys, and beat them when they ran races, she liked to be quiet. Nobody could sew and spin better than she did, and she was very fond of praying alone in church. She would even go away from the other children into lonely places, and implore God to have pity on France. The services in church, the singing and music, made her very happy, and when she heard the church bells across the fields, she would say her prayer. She was very kind, and would give up her bed to any poor traveller whom her father took in for a night, and would sleep beside the hearth She took care of the sick, and, if ever she had any money, she would spend it on Masses to be said in honour of God, and for the sake of men's souls.

So Joan lived till she was thirteen. She was a strong, handsome girl, beautifully made, with black hair. We do not know the colour of her eyes, probably brown or dark grey. A young knight wrote to his mother, when he first saw Joan, that she was "a creature all divine." Jean never sat to a painter for her portrait, though once she saw a kind of fancy picture of herself in the hands of a Scottish archer.

Young men do not say so much about a girl who is not beautiful, and indeed, armies do not rush together to follow a maiden with no good looks. But though Jean, when she came to command armies, liked to be well dressed, and to have fine armour, that was partly because she was a natural, healthy girl, and partly because she was a kind of banner for men to follow into fight, and banners ought to be splendid.

She took, no thought of her own beauty, and the young knights and squires who fought, later, under her flag, said that they looked on her as a sacred thing, and never dreamed of making love to her She let it be known that she would never marry any one, while the English were still in France. She was not a nun, and had not made a vow never to marry at all, but while her country was in danger she never thought of marriage; she had other things to do.

CHAPTER II. HOW THE VOICES CAME TO THE MAID

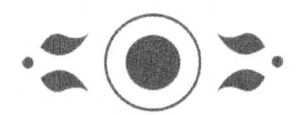

WHEN Joan was about thirteen a very wonderful thing happened to her. One day she and the other girls and boys were running a race for a crown of flowers. Joan was easily the winner, and as she was running, a child who was looking on cried, "Joan. I see you flying along without touching the ground." After the race Joan had a curious feeling as if she did not know where she was and then heard a young man's voice near her bidding her go home, for her mother needed her. She did not know who spoke; she thought it might be her brother, or one of her neighbours, so she ran home. She found that her mother had not sent for her, and she was going back to her friends, when a bright light like a shining cloud appeared to her, and a Voice told her to go and save France from the English. Till that hour she had been sorry for the sorrows in France, but as she was only a little girl, she had never thought that she could lead an army against the English.
This is the first account that people heard of the coming of the mysterious Voices to Jeanne: it was written down about four years after the Voices first came, and six weeks after Jean's first great defeat of the English (in May 1429). Two years later, after

Joan was a prisoner of the English, the French priests and lawyers who took the English side asked her thousands of questions about everything that she had done in her life, and the answers were written down in a hook, word for word. They asked her about these wonderful Voices. There were things that she refused to tell these priests and lawyers, but she did say this: —

"When I was about thirteen there came to me a Voice from God, teaching me how I was to behave and what I was to do. And the first time that Voice came, I was afraid. I was standing about the middle of the day, in summer, in my father's garden. The Voice came from the right hand, from where the church stands, and when it came I usually saw a great light on the side from which it spoke. The Voice told me to be a good girl and go to church, and go to save France. I said that I was only a poor girl, who could not ride or lead the soldiers in the wars," but the Voice kept on for years, telling her that she must go.

She not only heard Voices, but she saw shining figures of the Saints in heaven. She never would tell the lawyers much about how the Saints appeared to her, but said, "I saw them as clearly as I see you, and I used to cry when they went away. And I wished that they would take me with them where they went."

These Saints were St. Margaret, St. Catherine, and the Archangel St. Michael. When Joan spoke to her own friends about what she saw and heard they say that "she seemed marvelously happy, lifting her eyes to heaven." This is all that we know about these wonderful things which kept Joan company from the time when she was thirteen to the day of her death, when she was nineteen, advising her about what she was to do for the saving of France. If the Voices had not spoken to her often, she would never have gone to the wars, and for some years she told nobody about the Voices, and stayed at home in her village. Even when she went to the wars, her friends could not persuade her to say more than I have told you about these strange things. She said that she had a "council" which advised her in everything. If there was much noise in a room where she might be, she could not hear the Voices distinctly. Only one person said that he saw angels' faces in her company; none of her friends who knew her best saw or heard anything extraordinary. She very much disliked to speak about the Saints and Voices.

CHAPTER III. HOW THE MAID OBEYED THE VOICES

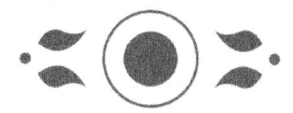

TIME went on, and the Dauphin, the rightful Prince of France, was more and more unfortunate. It is true that Henry V., the King of England, died. He was a great soldier, and his son was only a baby, but the war was carried on by the brother of the late King, the Duke of Bedford; by the Earl of Salisbury; by the famous Talbot; by Sir John Fastolf, and many other English generals. The Scots won a great victory over the English at Baugé bridge, where the Duke of Clarence, the brother of Henry V., was killed. But the French and Scots were beaten at Verneuil, where most of the Scots fell fighting bravely. However, a new army came from Scotland, under Stewart of Dam-ley, and still the war went on.

By that time the Dauphin only held France south of the great river Loire. The strongest place which was true to the Dauphin was the town of Orleans. If the English could once take that city, and fill it with previsions, and guns, and other weapons, the French could not hope to win it back again, and the English would overrun the whole of the centre and south of France, and drive the Dauphin out of his own country. He was very poor and very unhappy. He could scarcely pay his bootmaker, and as he was not a good fighting man, he lived here and there idly, at towns south of Orleans, such as Blois and Poitiers. He used to wonder whether he had not better give up the war and go to Spain or Scotland. Another thing made him miserable. He did not know for certain whether he had really the right to be King or not, as many people said that he was not truly the son of the last King of France.

In his distress he prayed, privately and in silence, that he might know whether or not he was the rightful prince, and ought to be crowned and anointed as King. But he told nobody about this, and lived as he best could, wandering from one town to another. Then he heard that his great city of Orleans was being besieged by the English, in the autumn of the year 1428. Orleans lies on the right bank of the river Loire, which here is deep, broad, and swift, with several islands in the middle of the current. The bridge was fortified, on the farther side, by two strong towers, called Les Tourelles, but the English took this fortification, and so the people of Orleans could not cross the river by the bridge, and they broke down an arch, that the English might not cross to them.

One day the English general came to this fort, at the time when the soldiers of both sides dined, to look out of a narrow window, and watch what was going on in the besieged town. Now it happened that a cannon lay, ready loaded, in a niche of the gate tower of Orleans that looked straight along the bridge to the Tourelles. The English general, the Earl of Salisbury, was peeping through the narrow window, thinking himself quite safe, as the French soldiers in Orleans had gone to dinner. But a small French boy went into the gate-tower of Orleans, and seeing a cannon ready loaded, he thought it would be amusing to set a light to the touch-hole. So he got a linstock, as it was called, lighted it, put it to the touch-hole, and fired off the cannon. The bullet went straight into the narrow window out of which the English general was peeping, and he fell back, mortally wounded.

This was a piece of good fortune for the French, but there were plenty of other English generals to take the place of Salisbury. The English built strong fortresses here and there, outside the walls and gates of the town, to prevent help and food and wine and powder from being brought to the besieged French. But the people of Orleans were brave, and were commanded by good officers, such as Dunois, young Xaintrailles. La Hire, a rough, swearing knight, and others who became true friends of Joan of Arc, and food was brought in easily enough.

The English had won so many battles that they despised the French, and so they did not take pains, and besides, they had not men enough to surround Orleans and prevent cattle being driven in from the country. The English seem to have had no more than four thousand soldiers. They were neither strong enough to take the town by storm, nor many enough to surround it and starve the French into showing the white flag, and giving up the place.

In fact, the English had been beating the French just because they believed they could beat them, and thought that one Englishman was as good as three Frenchmen at least. This was nonsense but, under Henry V., at Agincourt, a few English had beaten a great French army, because the French fought foolishly, trying to gallop to the charge over wet, heavy ploughed land, while the English arches shot them down in hundreds. But the French, you will see had learned the English way of fighting on foot, and could have held their own, if they had not lost confidence.

CHAPTER IV. HOW JOAN HEARD NEWS STRANGELY

JOAN, far away in Domremy, would hear of the danger in which Orleans lay, now and then, and her Voices kept insisting that she must go and drive away the English. She used to cry, and say that she would be quite useless, as she could not ride or fight, and people would think her mad, or bad, and laugh at her.

The Voices told her to go to the nearest strong-walled French town, Vaucouleurs, and ask the commander there, Robert de Baudricourt, to send her to the Dauphin, who was then far away, at Chinon, a castle on the Loire, south of Orleans. When she saw the King, she was to tell him that she had come to save France.

This seemed quite a mad proposal. Baudricourt was a greet, rough, sensible soldier, and how could Joan go to him with a message of this kind? He would merely laugh at the sunburned girl in her short red kirtle—a girl who, probably, had never spoken to a gentleman before.

Perhaps this was the hardest part of Joan's duty, for she was modest, and she was very quick to notice anything absurd and ridiculous. Now nothing could seem more laughable than the notion that a little country wench of sixteen could teach the French to defeat the English. But there was no help for it. The Voices, and the shining cloud, and the faces of Saints and angels came, several times every week, and a Voice said, "Daughter of God, go on! I will be with you."

Joan had an uncle who lived near Vaucouleurs, and she went to stay with him. It seems that she told him she must go to the Dauphin, and the first thing needful was to get Robert de Baudricourt to lend her a few men-at-arms, who would protect her on her long journey to Chinon. The uncle must have been very much astonished, but it seems that he believed in her, for he took her to Robert. Of course Robert laughed, and told Joan's uncle to take her away, and box her ears. But she came again, and then a priest wanted to exorcise her, that is to frighten the devil out of her, with religious services and holy water, as if she had been "possessed," like people in the New Testament. But Joan was not possessed, and the priest, after trying the holy water, could only say so.

By this time the month of February 1429 had come round. The besieged French in Orleans had now a great misfortune. The season of Lent was coming; that is, a time when they were not allowed to eat beef and mutton, but only fish, and eggs, and vegetables. Now a great number of waggons loaded with herrings were being sent to feed the English who were besieging Orleans. The general of the French in Orleans knew that, and he determined to send out soldiers to attack the English who would be guarding the long line of waggons full of herrings. They would wait for the English on the road, cut them up, and carry the fish into the town for their own use.

So a great many of the Scots and some French slipped out of Orleans by night, and went to a place called Rouvray, on the road by which the herrings were to pass. Here they were to be joined by another small French army, under a general named Clermont. So they reached Rouvray, where they did not find Clermont and his men, but did see the English soldiers far away, marching by the side of the long line of waggons.

Instead of waiting hidden under cover till the English passed, by, and then rushing among them unexpectedly, Stewart of Damley cried, "Charge!" and rode, with his lance in rest at the English front. The Scots were always in too great a hurry to fight. The English saw them, coming, arranged the heavy waggons in a square, and went inside the square, so that the Scots could not get at them. Safe behind their carts, the English archers shot down the Scots, who thought bows and arrows rather mean weapons, and wanted to cut down their enemies with the sword. But they could not reach the English; they fell in piles of slain men round the square, and Clermont, the French general who was to have joined them, would not fight, and took away his army. So very many brave Scots were killed, with Stewart of Darnley at their head, and the rest retreated sadly to Orleans, where they heard the English hurrahing in their camp.

This was called the battle of Rouvray, or the battle of the Herrings. It was fought on February 12, 1429. Now, on February 12, Joan went to Baudricourt, and told him that a terrible misfortune had happened that day to the army of the Dauphin, near Orleans. The news could not possibly reach Vaucouleurs for several days, for the distance between Vaucouleurs and Orleans is great, and the roads were dangerous, and might be beset by English soldiers and by robbers, who would stop messengers. Joan had been told of the defeat by her Voices.

At last, however, the bad news did come. Joan had been right, the French and Scots had been defeated on the day when she told Baudricourt of it, February 12.

So Baudricourt saw there was something uncommon in this country girl, who knew what was happening far away, and he lent her two young gentlemen and a few men-at-arms to guide her and guard her on her way to the Dauphin. Somebody gave her a horse, which, to the surprise of all men, she rode very well. She had her long black hair cut short and close, as soldiers wore it; she dressed in a grey doublet and black hose, like a boy (she wore this kind of dress till the end of her life); and then she rode through the gate of Vaucouleurs which is still standing, and away to seek the Dauphin. This was on February 23, 1429.

After riding for several days, Joan and her company reached a little town called Fierbois, near Chinon. Here was the chapel dedicated to St. Catherine of Fierbois, who was a favourite Saint of the French and Scots soldiers, and of Joan. In the chapel was a book in which the miracles of the Saint were written down. At this very time a Scottish archer, Michael Hamilton, from Shotts, was caught by some country people, and was hanged by them. During the night a voice came to the priest of the village, saying, "Go and cut down that Scot who was hanged, for he is not dead." However, the priest was sleepy, and he did not go. Next day was Easter Day, and the priest went to church and did the services. After that, he thought he might as well see about the Scot who was hanging from a tree, and seemed quite dead. To make certain, the priest took his penknife, and cut the dead man's toe. On this the man gave a kick, so the priest cut the rope, and took good care of Michael Hamilton. When he was able to ride, Michael went to this chapel of Fierbois, and took his oath that he had prayed to St. Catherine before he was hanged up, and now he came to thank her for his escape at her chapel. The book of the chapel is full of these strange stories, and probably some of them were read aloud to Joan, who could not read, and said that she "did not know A from B." She attended three Masses at Fierbois, and get some learned clerk to write a letter to the King, to say that she was coming. She also had a letter written to her father and mother, asking them to pardon her for going away without their permission. Her father she was to see once more, her mother she never saw again.

As to Michael Hamilton, you may believe his story or not, as you like. Many of the other stories told in the chapel book by Scots soldiers, and French men and women, are just as curious. I only know that the people made long journeys to thank Madame Saint Catherine in her church at Fierbois, and that their stories were written down in the book there.

CHAPTER V. HOW THE MAID SAW THE DAUPHIN

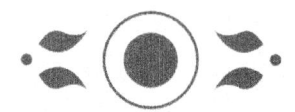

WHEN Joan reached Chinon, she was lodged with a lady who was very kind, and she waited to see the Dauphin. His advisers were not sure that he ought to see the Maid at all; but probably he was curious, and at last she was brought to the castle, and led up the stairs to a great hall, where were many men in splendid dresses. The castle is in ruins now, and the hall has no roof over it, but you can still go in and see the walls, and empty windows, and the great fireplace. A man plainly dressed was in the crowd of magnificent courtiers in silk and gold embroidery. Joan went straight up, and kneeling on one knee, said, "Fair Sir, you are the Dauphin to whom I am come." But the man pointed to a knight, very richly dressed, and said, "That is the King."
"No, fair Sir," said Joan; "it is to you that I am sent."

The Dauphin, for the man was the Dauphin, was surprised at this, for she had never seen him before. He allowed Jean to come to the castle and talk to him, but he was not sure that she was not an impostor, or a silly girl.

One day, however, she took him aside, into a corner where nobody could hear what they were talking about. When their conversation was ended, the Dauphin looked very grave, and Jeanne looked very glad. She had told him something that made him believe in her.

What had Joan told to the King? It was known at the time that she had told him something that amazed him, for it is mentioned in a letter written a few weeks later by Alan Chartier, a famous poet. But nobody knew the secret: Joan would never let any one know. When she was a prisoner among the English, the French-priests and lawyers tried to make her speak, but she would not. It was her King's secret.

Eight year's after Joan was dead, a very strange thing happened. A woman who said that Joan had not died, and that she was Joan, came to Orleans with Joan's brothers. The people of Orleans, who had known the Maid very well, believed that this woman was Joan come again, and feasted her and gave her presents. Then she was taken to the King. He himself was puzzled, and said, "Maid, my dear, I am glad to see you again. Do you remember the secret between you and me?"

Then this false pretender to be the Maid confessed that she knew nothing.

When the King was old, he revealed the secret to a friend.

On that day when they went apart together at Chinon. Joan reminded him of the secret prayer which, as I told you, the Dauphin had made when alone, asking that he might know whether he really was the son of the late King, and himself the rightful King of France.

"You are the rightful King," Joan said.

When the Dauphin heard her words, he made things go on quicker. Priests were sent to Joan's village to find out if she had been a good girl when she was at home.

Then she was taken to Poitiers, to be examined by many learned men, priests and lawyers. They tried to perplex her by their questions, but she was straightforward, and told them how the Voices had come to her. One man asked her to give a sign by working a miracle.

"I have not come to Poitiers to give signs." said Joan; "but let me go to Orleans, and you shall see what I will do."

She never professed to work miracles. She wanted to lead an army to Orleans, and the sign to be given was the defeat of the English, and the rescue of the besieged town.

For six weary weeks the learned men and priests examined Joan, and tried in every way to find some fault in her answers. At last they drew up a report and signed it, saying that "to doubt the Maid would be to resist the Holy Spirit." What they were afraid of all the time was that Joan might be advised by spirits, to be sure, but evil spirits or devils. The English and the French lawyers on the English side, declared that Joan was possessed by devils. They thought that, because they could not deny her powers; but, as she was not on their side, her powers could not come from God, but from Satan. To think in that way is common: people always believe that their own side is the right side. But nobody ever heard of evil spirits taking possession of any one who was really good; and no man could ever find any single bad thing in Joan the Maid.

So now the Dauphin began to collect an army to march with Joan to Orleans. Of course he ought to have done that before, even if there had been no Joan. It was a shameful thing that a strong town, full of brave men, should be taken by four thousand Englishmen, without an effort by the French to drive the English away. But the French had lost all heart and courage: the brave Danois himself said that a large force of French would run away from a little company of English. All that the French of the Dauphin's party needed was courage and confidence. As soon as they believed in Joan they were full of confidence. They could not turn their backs as long as a girl of sixteen ran forward in front of them, through the rain of arrows, and bullets, and cannon balls, waving her banner, and crying "Come on!"

At this time Joan prophesied that she would be wounded by an arrow at Orleans, but not to death. So a Flemish ambassador at Chinon wrote to the magistrates of his town at hone, and his letter was copied into the town council's book, before the Maid went to the war.

White armour was made for Joan to wear, and a Scottish painter made a banner with sacred pictures for her to carry: his daughter was a great friend of Joan.

The Maid said that, as for a sword, if they dug in the ground behind the altar at the chapel of St. Catherine, in Fierbois, they would find a buried sword, which she wished to carry; and it was found, old and rusty, with five crosses on the blade. The Duke of Alençon, a young cousin of the King's, who had been a prisoner of the English, saw Joan riding one day, and was so pleased with her grace and good horsemanship, that he gave her a very good horse, and became one of her best friends. "My fair Duke" was what she used to call him. Every one said that Joan's manners were as gentle and courteous as those of the greatest ladies, though she had been brought up in a poor cottage. Everything that she did was done in the best way and the noblest.

CHAPTER VI. HOW THE MAID RODE TO ORLEANS

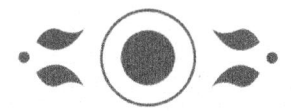

WHEN Joan's army was gathered, with plenty of good things, and powder and shot, in waggons, for the people of Orleans, she gave orders that no loose people should follow them. The soldiers must not drink and play dice and cards. They must pray, and must never swear. One of the generals, the brave La Hire, asked that he might be allowed one little oath, so she said he might swear "by his baton," the short staff which he carried as a leader. Then Joan mounted, and rode at the head of the amy out of the gate of Blois. The French Commander at Orleans, Danois, had sent to say that they must march up the bank of the Loire opposite to that on which Orleans stands, for the English were very strong, with many fortifications, on the road on the Orleans side, and would stop them. Dunois seems to have thought that Joan's army should go above the town, and be ferried across with the supplies for the city-for the English held the bridge—but that they could not cut their way through the main body cf the English army on the other side of the river. But to go straight through the English where they were strongest was what Joan had intended. Therefore she was angry when she arrived at the place where

Dunois was waiting for her, and saw that the river lay between her and the town of Orleans. You may think that her Voices should have told her that she was marching on the wrong bank of the river: however, they did not. She asked Dunois why he had ordered them to come by the road they took. She said, "I bring you better help than has ever come to any town or captain, the help of the King of heaven."

Dunois himself has left this account of what Joan said, and, as she was speaking, the wind changed. It had been blowing in such a way as to make it hard for the boats to carry Joan and the provisions across the river, but now it went about, and they crossed easily, some way above the town. As for the army, Joan ordered them back to Blois, to cross by the bridge there, and march to Orleans again, past the forts and through the midst of the English.

Once across the river, Joan mounted again, with her banner of Our Lord and the Lilies in her hand, and with Dunois at her side, and rode to the town. They passed an English fortress, the Church of St Loup, in safety, and the people came out to meet them. Night had fallen, and the people who crowded round the Maid were carrying torches. Ore of these set fire to the fringe of her banner and made her horse plunge; but she crushed out the flame with her left hand in its steel glove, and reined in her horse easily, while the people cheered, and the women wished to kiss her hand, which she did not like, thinking the honour too great. It was a beautiful sight to see the Maid ride into Orleans town. From that hour there was no more fear among the French.

Joan riding into Orleans under torchlight

Dunois said, "till that day, two hundred English could scatter eight hundred or a thousand of our men, but now they skulked in their forts and dared not come out against us." This is an extraordinary thing, for Talbot, who led the English, was the bravest of men, and was thought the greatest captain living. Jeanne sent to him a letter to bid him break up his camp and go away. The English laughed, and one day, when Joan went out to speak to them, they called her ill names, so that she wept for shame. But, somehow, the English had certainly lost heart, or they had some reason which we do not know, for merely defending their strong fortresses.

On the day after Joan entered Orleans she wanted Dunois to sally out of the town with his men and assail the English. He did not think it wise to do so and Joan went up to her own room. Suddenly she rushed down and asked her page why he had not told her that the French were fighting, she did not know where. It was at the fort and Church of St. Loup, which

Joan had passed on her way into Orleans. On this side, namely, farther up the river, above the town, the English were weakest, as they did not expect to be attacked on that side. The French were victorious: when they saw Joan ride up they were filled with courage. Joan saw a Frenchman strike down an English prisoner: she dismounted; laid the poor prisoner's head in her lap, and did her best to comfort him.

CHAPTER VII. HOW THE MAID SAVED ORLEANS

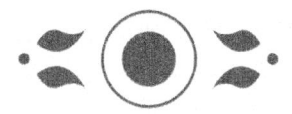

THE Dauphin had given Joan a gentle-man of good character to be with her always, and take care of her. This gentleman was named Jean d'Aulon, and, as he has left an account of what Joan did at Orleans, we give what he said. On the day after Joan took the fortress of St. Loup from the English, she led her men to attack another English work on the farther side of the river. They could not cross by the bridge, of course, for the English held the strong building, Les Tourelles, at the bridge end, the place where the Earl of Salisbury was killed by the cannon shot; moreover an arch of the bridge had been broken, lest the English should cross. So they went in boats to an island in the middle of the river, and then made a bridge of boats across the other branch of the Loire. But they found that the English had left the place which they meant to attack, and were in a much stronger fortress. The French, therefore, were returning to their boats, when the English rushed out of the second fortress to attack them when off their guard. But Joan and her friend La Hire, who had crossed the river with their horses, saw the English coming on, and put their lances in rest (a kind of support for the level spear), and spurred their horses at their enemies. The rest of the French followed Joan, and drove the English back into their fortress. Meanwhile d'Aulon, and a Spanish gentleman on the French side, took each other by the hand, and ran as fast as they could till they struck their swords against the outer fence, or strong wooden palisade of the English. But in the narrow gateway stood a tall and very strong Englishman, who drove back the French. So d'Aulon asked a Frenchman, a good shot, to aim at the Englishman, whom he killed, and then d'Aulon and the Spaniard ran into the gateway, and held it, while Joan and the rest of the French rushed in, and all the English were killed or gave themselves up as prisoners.

By this time the French army which went down to Blois to cross the bridge, had returned to Orleans, and gone past the English fortresses without being attacked. So there were now many fighting men in Orleans. Next day, therefore, Joan insisted that they should attack the strongest of all the English forts, Les Tourelles, at the end of the bridge farthest from the town. The generals thought this plan too dangerous, as the fortress was so strong; but no doubt Joan was right, because the English on the town side of the river could not cross over to help their countrymen. If they crossed in boats, they would be shot, and cut down as they landed. If the French generals did not understand that. Joan did. She was full of confidence. A man asked her to wait for breakfast, and offered her a big trout caught in the Loire. She said, "Keen it for supper. I will bring back an English prisoner to help to eat it. And I will come back by the bridge," Now the bridge, we saw, was broken.

D'Aulon heard her say this, and no doubt he wondered what she meant. He understood her, at night.

So Joan caused the gate to be thrown open, and the town's

people, who were very eager, rushed to the river bank, and crossed in boats. The regular soldiers followed, and all day long they attacked the walls, carrying ladders to climb then? with, while Joan stood under the wall, waving her banner, and crying "Forward!" But from behind the battlement, the English kept shooting with arrows and muskets, so that many of the French were killed, and a strong Englishman threw down the ladders as they were pushed to the top of the walls. There were five or six hundred of the best of the English in this castle, under two leaders whom the French call "Bumus" and "Glasidas." The name of "Glasidas" was Glasdaie; we do not know who "Bumus" was! So all day companies of the French and Scots, carrying ladders, and with banners flying, went down into the deep ditch below the wall, and were shot or driven out.

Now the great Dunois, the most famous of the French leaders, tells us what Joan did. It was about one o'clock in the afternoon, when the thing that she had prophesied happened to her. A bolt from an English cross-bow passed through her armour between the collar-bone and the shoulder-blade, and stood out six inches behind her shoulder. She was carried out of range, and the arrow was drawn out. Another witness says that a soldier wished to sing a magical song over the wound, to heal it, but she would not allow this to be done, and went back into the battle, hurt as she was. She cried a little.

They fought on: they had begun in the early morning, and it was eight o'clock, and past sunset, when Dunois said that they could not take the fort that day, and wished to call off the soldiers from the ditch. But Joan came to him, and asked him to wait a little while. She mounted her horse, and rode to a vineyard, and there she prayed, "for half a quarter of an hour." Then she rode back, and went through the hail of shot and arrows to the edge of the ditch, while d'Aulon covered her, he says, with his shield. She saw that a soldier had taken her standard into the ditch. She seized the standard, and it waved so that all her men saw it, and rushed up; "we shall take the fort," said Joan, "when my standard touches the wall." The wind blew the banner fringe against the wall, and the French made one more rush, they climbed the ladders, they tumbled into the fort, and the English were slain or taken, and Glasdale, their leader, who tried to cross to another tower by a plank, fell into the river and was drowned.

Then Joan crossed back to Orleans by the bridge, as d'Aulon heard her say that she would, when she set out in the morning. For the town's people laid a beam across the broken arch, and on this she walked over, after winning so great a victory by her own courage. For Dunois says that the English were terrified when they saw her under the wall again, in the growing darkness, and that they had no more heart to fight.

Joan was very tired: she had her wound dressed by a surgeon, and, for supper, she had four or five little pieces of toast, dipped in weak wine and water: that was all she ate, Dunois says, all that long day.

Early next morning the English left their forts, and drew up in line of battle. Joan had put on a very light shirt of mail, made of steel rings, because her wound did not permit her to wear the usual armour made of heavy steel plates. She said that the English must be allowed to go away, and must not be attacked.

Thus the town of Orleans was delivered on 8th May, and ever since, to this day, they keep a festival on 8th May in every year, ard rejoice in honour of the Maid. All the expense and labour of the English in the seven months' siege had been turned to waste by Joan in four days, France was free, south of the Loire, and Joan had kept her word, she had shown a sign at Orleans.

It sounds like a fairy-tale, but it certainly happened. Joan made the French able to do what they did merely by giving them courage. Her army would not have come together if she had not given them something to believe in-herself. She thought that she led about 10,000 men; but it is not easy to be sure of the numbers. The English, if they were only 4000, could not resist the new army and the old garrison of Orleans, if the French had faith in themselves; and Joan gave them faith. At the same time the English seem to have arranged their army in a very foolish way. About 1000 were or the farther side of a river which the 3000 on the right bank could not, or did not try to cross, to help their friends. The larger part of the English army might have attacked one of the gates of Orleans, and frightened Joan's army, who would have come back across the river to defend the town. The English in the fortress at the farther end of the bridge would then have been safe. But the English on the right bank did nothing at all, for some reason which we do not understand.

CHAPTER VIII. HOW THE MAID TOOK THE TOWN OF JARGEAU

AFTER Orleans was quite safe, and when Talbot had led the English army to the town of Meun, Joan wanted to take the Dauphin to Rheims, to be crowned and anointed with the holy oil, and made King in earnest. But the way was long, and the road passed through towns which were held by friends of the English. So the Dauphin loitered about in pleasant castles near the Loire, in the bright May weather, and held councils, and wondered what he ought to do. Then Joan rode with the brave Dunois to Loches where the Dauphin was. Some lords and priests were in the room with him, but Joan went straight in, and knelt before him, saying, "Fair Dauphin, do not hold so many weary councils, but come to Rheims, and take your crown."

So they said that they would think about it, but was it safe to leave English armies behind them, at Meun, where Talbot was, and at Jargeau, where the Earl of Suffolk was the English captain? Joan said that she and the young Duke of Alençon would make their minds easy on that point, and would begin by taking Jargeau, where the French, without Joan, had fought already and been beaten. The Duke was newly married to a young wife, who was anxious about him, but Joan said, "Madam, I will bring back the Duke to you, safe and well!" So they rode away, six hundred lances, with some infantry, and slept in a wood. The Duke of Alençon has left an account of all that they did. Next day Dunois and other captains joined them with another six hundred lances, so that, with the infantry, they would be about five thousand men. Some of the captains thought they were not strong enough, as Jargeau had thick walls and rowers, and cannon. But Joan insisted on fighting and first she led her men to drive the English from the houses lying under the walls on the outside, which is dangerous fighting, as all the garden walls would protect English cross-bowmen, and men with muskets, who could shoot in safety, many of them from windows of houses, at the French in the open. The French, however, drove the English from the houses and gardens, and brought up their cannon, and fired at the town.

In these days cannon were small, and shot small balls, which did not carry far, and could do no damage to thick stone walls. There were no shells, which explode, but there were a few very large iron guns, like Mons Meg in Edinburgh Castle. Out of these they shot huge, heavy stone balls, and if one of them fell into a street, and broke, the splinters flew about dangerously. But, somehow, they seldom did much harm, besides Joan's army had none of these great guns, which are not easily dragged about.

So for days the French fired at the town, and it is to be supposed that they broke a hole, or breach, in a part of the wall, for they decided to rush in and take the place sword in hand.

"Forward, fair Duke!" said Joan to the Duke of Alençon, who rather thought that they had not made a good enough breach in the wall. "You know that I told the Duchess I would bring you back safe? But do not stand there," she said, "or that English cannon on the wall will kill you."

The Duke moved from the place where he was, and a gentleman named da Luce went to it, and was killed.

So Joan saved the Duke, as she had promised.

Then they ran together to the wall, and Jean was climbing up a ladder, when a heavy stone thrown by the English struck her helmet, and she fell.

She rose again at once, crying, "Forward, we shall take them all," and the English ran through the streets to the bridges, the French following and cutting them down, or taking them prisoners. It is said that the Earl of Suffolk surrendered to Joan, as "the bravest woman in the world." If this is true, she might have made a great deal of money out of his ransom, that is, the price which a prisoner paid for his freedom. There is another story that Suffolk was taken by a squire, and that he dubbed him knight before he surrendered as it was more honourable to yield to a knight. This is more likely to be true, for the English thought that Joan was a witch. Now, as Suffolk was general of all the English forces on the Loire he would not choose to surrender to a lass of sixteen, whether he believed in witches or not Besides, he could not dub Joan a knight.

CHAPTER IX. HOW JOAN DEFEATED THE ENGLISH IN FAIRFIELD

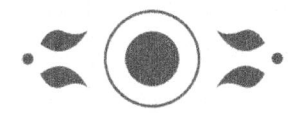

THE Maid had now driven the English away from Orleans, and had taken a strong town which they held, a thing the French, without her, had failed to do. She was next to beat their army In the open country and in fair field. We know most about this battle from a book written by a gentleman named Pierre de Cagny, who rode with the Duke of Alencon and knew what happened, and wrote all down very soon afterwards. He says that the Maid placed a garrison of soldiers to keep Jargeau, and then rode to Orleans with the Duke, where the townspeople gave a great feast to her and her friends. But she did not stay long to be petted and praised at Orleans. In the evening she said to the Duke, "I am going, after dinner tomorrow, to see the English at Meun. Have the men ready to march." She easily made Meun surrender, and then her guns fired at the town of Beaugency.

Then news came to Joan that the whole English army, under Talbot and Sir John Fastolf (who cannot be Sir John Falstaff in Shakespeare, for the fat knight was dead), were marching against her. Now Sir John Fastolf, though a very brave captain, thought, like the fat knight, that "discretion was the better part of valour." He wished to be cautious, and to avoid a battle, for he saw that the French were in high spirits, while the English soldiers had lost heart. This is told in the book written by a knight named Jean de Wavrin, a Burgundian. He was, like all of them of Burgundy, on the English side, and he rode under the banner of Sir John Fastolf.

I tell you generally how we come to know the things done by the Maid, to show that the story is true, as the people who described it were present, and saw what happened.

The other English captains thought Sir John rather too cautious, and Talbot said. "By St George. I will fight if I have only my own few men with me!" Next morning the English rode out with banners flying, and again Sir John said that they were too few, and that they were risking all that Henry V. had gained in France. But Talbot and the rest would not listen to him, so the trumpets blew, and the horsemen rode on towards Meun, which Joan had taken. When they came to a place about three miles from Meun, and three from Beaugency, they saw the banner of the Maid, with Our Lord and the Lilies of France, and the banners of the Duke of Alençon, and Dunois, and La Hire, and young Pothon de Xaintrailles, a very gallant boy, waving over the ranks of 6000 men.

The English then did what Henry V. had taught them to do. They dismounted from their horses to fight on foot, and made each bowman plant his sharp stake in front of him, to stop a cavalry charge. This plan usually succeeded. The French were fond of charging with their cavalry at full speed, and then were usually shot down in heaps by the English bowmen, whom they could not reach, as they were safe behind their fence of pikes. Then the dismounted English would rush out, sword in hard, among the disordered French cavalry.

You see this was much like part of the battle of Waterloo, when the French cavalry many times rode at the English squares, and could not break through the bayonets, while the English were shooting at them not very straight!

By this plan of fighting the English had often defeated the French, and usually defeated the Scots, who generally made a wild rush at them. At the battle of Dupplin, soon after Robert Bruce died, the English archers shot from each flank till the Scots, as they charged, fell dead in heaps as high as a tall spear. But Dunois, and the fair Duke, and the Maid knew this plan. They sent a herald to bid the English go home to bed; it was late; "tomorrow we shall have a nearer view of each other."

The English, therefore, went off to Meun, where nobody resisted them except the French soldiers who guarded the bridge over the Loire. The English meant to beat the French from the bridge with their cannons, cross the river, and march to help their friends in Beaugency, which had not yet yielded to Joan. The English would thus take Joan's army between two fires, that of Beaugency, and that of Talbot's army.

But that very night the English in Beaugency lost heart, and yielded to the Maid, being allowed to march away with their arms and horses. Jean now bade the French captains go with her army, and look for Talbot's and Fastolfs force, who would hear of the surrender of Beaugency, and retreat to Paris through the country called La Beauce.

"But how are we to find the English?" the French leaders asked Joan: for they would be in a wild, empty country covered with forests.

"Ride forth," she said; "we shall take them all. As to finding them, you shall have a good guide!"

They had a strange guide, as you shall hear.

The English were marching along, in front was their advanced guard, under a knight who carried a white banner. Next came the guns, with the waggons full of provisions. Third was the main body of the army, under Talbot and Fastolf; and last rode the rear-guard. When they were near a place called Pathay, their scouts galloped in, with news that they had seen the French army. The English halted, and sent out more scouts, who rode back with the same news.

So Talbot sent his advanced guard, the guns, and the waggons behind some tall hedges. The main body of the English army was being placed at the end of a long lane between two thick hedges, and Talbot set five hundred of his best archers to lurk behind these hedges, between which the French would have to pass before they could attack the centre of his forces. If the French once entered this long lane, they would be shot down, and fall into such confusion among their own fallen men and wounded horses, that they would neither be able to go forward nor back, and would all be killed or taken prisoners.

The French of Joan's army could not see what Talbot was doing, and the trap he had set, nor where his army was, the country being covered with wood and bracken, and the English being concealed by the swelling of the ground. However, they rode forward fast, and would bare been between the fire of the two hidden lines of English bowmen in a minute, when, lo and behold! they had "the good guide" that Joan had promised them! As they rode they roused a stag from the bracken where he was lying: the stag rushed forward into the concealed lines of English archers, and they, being hunters like Robin Hood's men, forgot to lie still, and raised a view halloo, and shot at the stag. Then the foremost riders of the French heard them, and knew where the English were lying in ambush. When Talbot saw that his ambush was found out, he hurried the main body of hie army up to the hedges. Sir John Fastolf's men were spurring their horses on to join their advanced guard, but the English knight of the white banner who led thought that Fastolf's cavalry were French, and that the French were attacking: his men both in front and rear, So he and his company ran away leaving: the lane unguarded. Thus, when the battle began, Talbot was defeated by Joan's cavalry, and taken prisoner, and 2200 of the English were killed or taken before Fastolf came up. He and his horsemen then rode away as fast as they could, to save their lives, and for this behaviour Sir John got into very deep disgrace, though, according to Wavrin, who was with him, he really could have done nothing else, as Talbot was beaten before he could arrive. As Wavrin had taken part in the flight, he had to make as good a defence of Sir John as he could. At all events, Joan and her party won a very great victory, the battle of Pathay.

Now look what Joan had done. She drove the English from Orleans on 8th May. Then the Dauphin took to holding long and weary councils, and she did not get another chance to fight the English till about 4th June, so nearly a month of her one year of time was wasted. On 11th June she took Jargeau, on 15th June she took Meun, on 17th June she took Beaugency, and on 18th June she destroyed Talbot's chief army at Pathay!

The Duke of Alencon tells us that he himself heard Joan tell the Dauphin, again and again, that "she would only last for a year, or not much longer, and that he must make haste." She had four things to do, she said: to drive the English in flight, to crown the King at Rheims, to deliver Orleans, and to set free the Duke of Orleans, who was a prisoner in England.

She did drive the English in flight, she did save Orleans, she did have the Dauphin crowned. But the French would not make haste. The Dauphin was always slow, and the stupid political advisers who never fought but only talked, made him more slow, and, when Joan's year was over, for her prophecy was true, she was taken prisoner by the English. Therefore they were not driven quite out of France till about twenty years or more after the end of the year of Joan the Maid. It was not her fault. She knew that her time was short, and she told them to make haste. When she was asked how she knew things that were to happen, she said that her Voices told her, "my Council," she called them. But there was a French noble, La Tremoïlle, the King's favourite, and he was jealous of Jean and Dunois and the Constable of Brittany, an enemy of his, who had now come to ride under Joan's flag.

This Tremoille, and others, did not want to fight, and hoped to make friends with the Duke of Burgundy, whose array, though really French, fought on the side of the English. Now the one chance was to keep hitting the English hard and often, while they were shaken by their defeats, and before they had time to bring a new host from home. In England there was an army ready, which had been collected by Cardinal Beaufort, to fight the Hussites, a kind of warlike Protestants who were active in Germany. As soon as Joan had beaten the English at Orleans, they made up their minds to send this new army of theirs to protect Paris, where most of the people, and the University, were on the English side. They also made an arrangement with James I. of Scotland, so that they had nothing to fear from the Scots coming over the Border to attack them. The English were able to do all this because La Tremoïlle and his friends advised the Dauphin to loiter about, instead of making haste, as Joan desired, to keep on beating the English.

CHAPTER X. HOW JOAN LED THE DAUPHIN TO BE CROWNED

We may think that Joan's best plan would have been to attack the English in Paris at once, while they were still in a fright, after their great defeat at Pathay. But she thought that if the Dauphin was once crowned, and anointed with the holy oil, at Rheims, the French who were of the English party would join him more readily. Robert the Bruce, in the same way, had himself crowned at Scone, which, in Scotland, was the usual place for coronations, when he had only very few followers, and very little chance of beating the English. Rheims, as you can sec on the map, is a long way farther from Orleans than Paris, on the north-east.

But Joan had made up her mind to drag the Dauphin to Rheims to be crowned.

The Dauphin was lingering at Gien, which is some distance south of Orleans, instead of being at the head of his army, and in the front of the fighting, where he should have been. His lazy and cowardly favourites told him that it was a long way to Rheims, and on the road there were several towns with strong walls, and castles full of Englishmen and Burgundians, who would not let him pass.

Joan answered that she knew this very well, and cared nothing about it: all the towns and castles would yield and open their gates. So she left the Dauphin to do as he pleased, and went away with her company into the country. The Dauphin had no money to pay his troops, but men-at-arms came in, hundreds of them, saying that they would fight for the love of the Maid and of chivalry. No doubt they would have been very glad to crown her, in place of the stupid Dauphin, but the French law did not allow it; and Joan wanted nothing for herself, only to make France free, and go back to her mother, as she said. However, the Dauphin, who was grateful in his lazy way, made her and her brothers, Peter and John, nobles, and gave her a coat-of-arms, a sword supporting the Crown, with the Lilies of France on each side, and changed their name to du Lys. But Joan never used her coat-of-arms, but bore a Dove, silver, on a blue shield. Her brothers were with her, and seem to have fought very well, though in most ways they were quite ordinary young men.

When Joan went away, the Dauphin made up his mind at last to march to Rheims, going first to Troyes, a strong town on the road. All the castles and fortresses on the way, instead of resisting him, submitted to him, as Joan had said that they would. At Troyes, where he came on 8th July, the English garrison, and the people of the town who were on the English and Burgundian side, wanted to oppose him. They fought on the 8th and 9th of Jury. The Dauphin's advisers did not want to fight, the brave Dunois tells us, but Jean said, "Gentle Dauphin, bid your army besiege the town, and do net hold these long councils, for in three days I will bring you into the town." Then down she went to the great ditch or fosse round the town, and worked harder, says Dunois, than two or three of the most famous knights could have done. The people of Troyes then yielded to Joan, and they had a great feast in the city, which they needed, for the army had been living on soup made from the beans in the fields.

Then they went on to Rheims, and the Archbishop and all the people came out to meet them, with shouts of joy. On 17th July the Dauphin, with Joan and all his nobles, went to the Cathedral, and there he was crowned and anointed, and made King in earnest, Joan standing beside him with her banner in her hand. This was her happiest day, perhaps, and the last of her great days. She had done so much! In the beginning of May there was every chance that the English would take Orleans, and sweep across the Loire, and seize all France, and drive the Dauphin into Spain, or across the sea to Scotland, and France would have been under the English for who knows how long. But in two months Joan had driven the English behind the walls of Paris, and her Dauphin was King in deed.

Then the Maid knelt at the King's feet and wept for joy, in the great Cathedral, among the splendid nobles, and the lights, and the bright-coloured coats-of-arms, and the sweet smoke of incense.

"Gentle King," she said, calling him "King" for the first time, "now is the will of God fulfilled!" and the knights themselves wept for joy.

Somewhere in the crowd was an elderly countryman in his best clothes. Joan's father, whom now she saw for the first time since she left her village, and for the last time in her life. The King asked her to choose a gift and reward, and she asked that the people of her village, Domremy, should be free from paying taxes, and they were made free, and never paid taxes again, for three hundred years. On the books of the accounts of money paid by every town and village of France is written, after the names of Domremy and the village nearest it, Greux, Nothing. For the Sake of the Maid.

The paper in which the King ordered that they should pay nothing may still be seen, dated the last of July 1429.

How glad the people at Domremy must have been when Joan's father came home with the good news!

This was the last glad day of the Maid.

As she rode to Rheims, some people from Domremy met her and asked her if she was afraid of nothing.

"Of nothing but treachery," she said, and, from this day, she met treachery among the King's advisers, who held long councils, and did not fight.

As she rode from Rheims towards Paris, the people shouted round her, and she said that they were kind people, and she would like to be buried in their cathedral—she, who was never to be buried in the earth.

"Joan," said the Archbishop, "in what place do you expect to die?"

"Where God pleases, for of that hour and that place I know nothing more than you do. But would to God that now I might take off my armour, and go home to my father and mother," for, as she had seen her father, she was longing for her mother more than ever.

After this, the people about the King-, and the King himself, did not obey Joan, and all went wrong.

CHAPTER XI. HOW THE MAID WAS BETRAYED AT PARIS

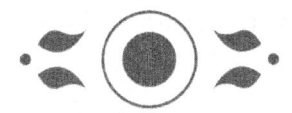

THE French should have followed the Maid straight to Paris, as she bade them do. But they went here and went there, and one day their army and that of the Duke of Bedford met, but did not fight; and another day there were skirmishes between the English and the Scots, "who fought very bravely," says the Burgundian knight, Enguerrand de Manstrelet, who wrote a history of those times. The strong town of Compiègne, which had often been taken and retaken, yielded to Joan's army, and the King stayed there, doing nothing, which was what he liked, and the Duke of Burgundy gave him excuses for loitering by sending ambassadors, and pretending that he would give up Paris, for at this time there was no English garrison there. The poor people of the town were on the side of Joan and the King, and now, when the English were out of the great city, was the time to take it. But the King kept hoping to make peace with the Duke of Burgundy, so Joan, with her friend the Duke of Alençon, went to Saint Denis, quite close to Paris, where the Kings of France used to be buried: Saint Denis was the Saint of France, as Saint George was the Saint of England, and Saint Andrew of Scotland. There fought the Duke and the Maid, but the King came on very slowly, while Joan was in the front of battle every day, at one gate of Paris or another. At last, by often going to him, and urging him to come, Alençon brought the King to Saint Denis, but not before a strong new English army had arrived in the town, of which the walls and towers were very high and thick, and the fosses broad and deep, and full of water.

Then Joan led on her men and the Duke's, with her banner in her hand, and cried them on to break down a gate called the Porte St. Honoré.

Percival de Cagny, who rode under the standard of Alençon, was in the battle, and he says, "The fight was long: and fierce, and it was wonderful to hear the noise of guns and culverins from the walls, and to see the arrows fly like clouds. Few of those who went down into the dry ditch with the Maid were hurt, though many others were wounded with arrows and stone cannon balls, but, by God's grace and the Maid's favour, there were none but could return without help. We fought from noon till darkness began. After the sun set, the Maid was wounded by a bolt from a cross-how in the thigh, but she only shouted louder to 'come on and the place was ours.' But when it was dark and all were weary, men came from the King and brought her up out of the ditch against her will."

Next day the Maid rose early, and went to the Duke of Alençon, who never failed her. The trumpets blew, and a new ally came, the Baron de Montmorency, with sixty gentlemen and their men-at-arms, and they were riding to attack Paris again when the King sent messengers to forbid them to do as their hearts desired. So they had to go to see him at Saint Denis. But the Duke of Alencon was having a bridge of wood thrown across the river Seine, at a new place, and they meant to cross by that bridge next day, and attack Paris again.

Shameful to say, the King had that bridge taken to pieces during the night, and when Joan and the Duke led their men there next day, they found only the river, which they could not ford. So the King of France saved Paris from d'Alençon and the Maid.

Richard I. of England would have battered down the Paris gate with his own battle-axe; Henry V. or James IV. of Scotland, or Prince Charlie, would have been, foremost in the fight; but this King of France, Charies VII., unworthy of his country and his ancestors, sneaked off to his pretty little town of Gien, on the Loire.

"And thus was the will of the Maid broken, and the army of the King," says Percival de Cagny.

The Duke of Alencon kept his men together, and told the King that, if he would let the Maid ride with him, they would march into Normandy, and attack the English where they were strongest. But the King would not hear of it, and the Maid, with almost a broken heart, hung up her armour at the altar of Saint Denis, in his Cathedral. Half of her year was spent, and the King made her stay with him in the towns on the Loire, when he might have been in Paris, his capital, if he had only trusted Joan.

In the meantime the English retook some of the French towns that Joan had given to the King, and seized her sacred armour in the Church of Saint Denis, and punished and plundered the people, who were worse off than before, while the Maid was only allowed now and then to attack the English, and defeat them in the old way.

CHAPTER XII. HOW THE MAID TOOK CERTAIN TOWNS

THE wise King had arranged with the Duke of Burgundy that they two should be at peace till Easter, 1430; while he might fight the English as much as he liked, which was, not at all.

Now the English let the Duke of Burgundy be Governor of Paris. It was always Paris that the Maid wished to take for her King, as it was the greatest city and the capital of France. But the King said she must not attack Paris, for it was now under the Duke of Burgundy, not under the English. All this was mere pretence, to avoid fighting. Jean's aim was to turn the English and their child King, Henry VI., out of her country; and the English were not likely to go out till they were driven out.

The English still held towns on the river Loire, such as St. Pierre-le-Moustier and La Charité. Joan went to Bourges and gathered an army, with a gentleman named d'Elbret to help her, and besieged the town of St. Pierre-le-Moustier. When they had battered the walls for some time with their guns, and made a breach, the French tried to rash through it; but the English were too strong and too many, and drove them out At this time Joan's Master cf the Household, d'Aulon, who had been with her at Orleans, was wounded in the heel by an arrow, and he could not walk without crutches. He saw that while the rest of the French had retired out of shot from the breach, Joan was there almost alone, with a very small company. D'Aulon therefore got a horse, and rode to her to ask her to come out of danger. "What are you doing here alone?" he asked her. She took off her helmet and said, "I am not alone; here I have with me fifty thousand of my own" (by which she seems to have meant an invisible army of Angels); "and will not leave this place till I take the town." D'Aulon told her that she had but four or five men with her, to which she only answered by bidding him make her army bring faggots of wood to fill up the ditch with, that they might cross to the town. Then she shouted in a loud voice:—

"Bring up faggots, all of you!" and they obeyed, filled up the ditch, attacked the breach in the wall again, rushed through, beat the English, and took the town.

This was just like what Joan had done when her army was on the point cf retreating from the attack on Les Tourelles, at Orleans. "One charge more" was what she called for, and her men were inspired with courage, while the English were terrified by their refusal to be beaten. This was the last time that Joan led the French to such a victory. She besieged another town, La Charité, which was held by Burgundians, but the King did mot send food enough for her men, and she had to go away unsuccessful.

About this time she was troubled by a woman called Catherine of La Rochelle, a married woman, who declared that a lovely lady came to her at night, dressed all in doth of gold, and told her where treasures of money were hidden, which were much needed for the wars. Jean said that she must see this wonderful lady before she could believe in her, and she sat up all night with Catherine; but the lady never came. Joan told Catherine to go back to her husband and her children, and mind her own affairs. There were several people who went about saying that they had visions; but they were of no use, for, visions or none, they had not Joan's courage and wisdom. It is true that Catherine might have said to Joan, "You can't see my golden lady, but I can't see your Saints, nor hear your Voices." The difference was that Joan's Saints and Voices had enabled her to do a great many wonderful things, while Catherine's golden lady never led to the finding of treasures or anything else that was of any use.

CHAPTER XIII. HOW THE VOICES PROPHESIED EVIL

THE end of the year of the Maid was at hand. She had often said that she would last but a year, or little more, counting from May 1429.

Perhaps you remember that the King had made a truce with the Burgundians—an useless truce, for the Burgundians went on fighting, not under their own flag, but under the Leopards of England. The King, as usual, was loitering about, doing nothing. Joan heard, in spring 1430, that three or four hundred English were crossing the Isle of France, which is not a real island, but a district of that name. She was then at Lagny, on the river Marne, not far from Paris. So she rode out from Lagny to meet them, with a gentleman whom the French called "Quenede." Can you guess what "Quenede" means? He was Sir Hugh Kennedy, of the great Kennedy clan in Callaway and Ayrshire. He had fought at the Battle of the Herrings and at Orleans, and he made a good deal of money in France, so that, when he went back to Scotland, he was called "Hugh come wi' the Penny."

When Joan, with her French and Scots, came in sight of the enemy, the English drew themselves up on foot, along the side of a hedge, and Joan and the rest charged them, some on foot, some on horse, and there was hard fighting, for the numbers were about equal But at last all the English were kil'ed or taken prisoners. There was also taken a robber knight, Franquet d'Arras, who was tried for his crimes and put to death, and the English party among the French thought it very wicked in Jean to allow the rogue to be punished.

In Easter Week Joan was at Melun one day, examining the ditch round the walls to see that it was in good order. Then suddenly the Voices of St. Catherine and St. Margaret spoke to her, and said that she should be taken prisoner before Midsummer day, "and thus it needs must be," and that she was to be resigned to this, and God would help her.

Often after this terrible day the Voices made the same prophecy, but they would never tell her the time and the hour. She prayed that she might die in that hour, for the English had often threatened her that they would burn her as a witch, if they caught her. Often she asked the Voices to warn her of the hour of her capture, for she would not have gone into battle on that day. But they would not tell her, and, after that, she did what the Captains of her party thought best, and it seems that, as to where or when she was to fight, she had no advice from the Voices. But she fought on as bravely as ever, and this was the bravest thing that ever was done by any one. For it was not as if the Voices had said that she should be killed in battle, of which she had no fear. But they said she was to be captured, and she knew that meant she was to be burned alive.

Nobody but Joan would have gone on risking herself every day, not to danger of war, which is the duty of every soldier, but to the death by fire. If any one says that the Voices were only her fancy, and her fear taking a fanciful shape, we must reply that, whatever they really were, she believed all that they said, and thought that they were the voices of her sisters, the Saints. Thus the end of Joan was the most glorious thing in her glorious life, for many could be brave enough when the Saints prophesied victory, but only she could give her body to be burned for her country.

CHAPTER XIV. HOW THE MAID WAS TAKEN

WE have heard how the town of Compiègne came over to Joan and the King, after the coronation at Rheims. The city had often been taken and retaken, and hold by both sides. But now they made up their minds that, come what might, they would be true to France, and now, in May, the English and Burgundians besieged Compiègne with a very large army.

Joan, who was at Lagny, heard of this, and she made up her mind to help the good and loyal town, or perish with it. She first tried to cut the roads that the Duke of Burgundy used for his soldiers and supplies of food, but she failed to take Soissons and Pent l'Évêque, and so shut the Duke off from his bridges over the rivers. So she rode into Compiègne under cloud of night, with her brother Pierre, and two or three hundred men. This was before dawn, on May 23.

The town of Compiègne is on the left bank of the river Oise. Behind the town was a forest, through which Joan rode, and got into the town, to the great joy of the people. From Compiègne to the right bank of the Oise, where the English and Burgundians had their camps, there was a long bridge, fortified, that led into a great level meadow, about a mile broad. In wet weather the meadow was often under water from the flooded river, so a causeway, or raised road, was built across it, high and dry. At the end of the causeway, farthest from Compiègne was the village of Margny, with the steeple of its church, and here a part of the Burgundian army was encamped. Two miles and a half farther on was the village of Clairoix, where lay another part of the Burgundian force. About a mile and a half to the left of the causeway was the village of Venette, which was held by the English, and, about three miles off, was Coudun, where the Duke of Burgundy himself had his quarters. There were very large forces in front, and on the side, of the only road by which Joan could get at them, with her own men, only three hundred, probably, and any of the townspeople who liked to follow her on foot, with clubs and scythes, and such weapons.

Thus it was really a very rash thing of Joan to lead so few men, by such a narrow road, to attack the nearest Burgundians, those at Margny, at the end of the causeway. The other Burgundians, farther off, and the English from Venette, quite near, and on Joan's left flank, would certainly come up to attack her, and help their friends at Margny. She would be surrounded on all sides and cut off, for the garrison of Compiègne stayed in the town, under their general, de Flavy, who was a great ruffian, but a brave man, and loyal to France.

Why Joan, about five o'clock in the evening of May 23. rode out with her little force, crossed the bridge, galloped down the causeway, and rode through and through the Burgundians at Margny, we do not know. Her Voices seem to have ceased to give her advice, only saying that she would certainly be captured. Perhaps she only meant to take Margny; though it is not easy to understand how she expected to hold it, when the whole Burgundian and English armies came up to recover it, as they would certainly do. If she aimed at more, her charge was very brave but very ill-judged. Joan said that her Voices did not tell her to make her desperate sally; it was her own idea.

Nearly seventy years afterwards, two very old men said that, when they were young at Compiègne, they heard Joan tell a crowd of children, before she rode out, that "I am betrayed, and soon will be delivered to death. Pray God for me, for I shall never again be able to help France and the King." One of the men was ninety-eight, so he would be quite twenty-eight when he heard Joan say this; if he really did hear her But, long before men are ninety-eight, or even eighty-six, line the other man, they are apt to remember things that never happened. But Joan may have told children, of whom she was very fond, that she knew she was soon to be taken.

Her enemies declared that she said she would take the Duke of Burgundy himself, but as he was several miles away, in the middle of a large army, while she had only three hundred of her own men, this cannot be true. Probably she only meant to break up the Burgundians at Margny, and show that she was there, to encourage the people at Compiègne.

Her own account is that she charged the Burgundians at Margny, the nearest village, and drove them twice back to Clairoix, where they were reinforced by the great Burgundian army there, and thrust her back to the middle of the causeway, where she turned again, charged them, and made them retreat. But then the English came up from Venette, on her flank, and came between her and the bridge of Compiègne, and she leaped her horse off the raised causeway into the meadow, where she was surrounded, and pulled off her horse and taken, though she would not surrender. No doubt she hoped that, as she refused to surrender, she would be killed on the spot. When they cried to her to yield she said, "I have given my faith to another than you, and I will keep my oath to Him," meaning Our Lord.

Joan taken at Compiègne

But she was too valuable to be killed. The captors might either get a great ransom, a king's ransom, or sell her to the English to burn. The French would not pay the ransom, and Jean de Luxembourg, who got possession of her, sold her to the English. The Burgundian historian, who was with the Duke, and did not see the battle, says, "the English feared not any captain, nor any chief in war, as they feared the Maid."

"She had done great deeds, passing the nature of woman." Says another Burgundian writer: "She remained in the rear of her men as their captain, and the bravest of all, there, where fortune granted it, for the end of her glory, and for that last time of her bearing arms."

But, indeed, her glory never ceased, for in her long, cruel imprisonment and martyrdom, she showed mere courage than any man-at-arms can display, where blows are given and taken.

CHAPTER XV. THE CAPTIVITY OF THE MAID

WE might suppose that there was not a rich man in France, or even a poor man, who would not have given what he could, much or little, to help to pay the ransom of the Maid. Jean de Luxembourg only wanted the money, and, as she was a prisoner of war, she might expect to be ransomed like other prisoners. It was the more needful to get the money and buy her freedom, as the priests of the University of Paris, who were on the English side, at once wrote to Jean de Luxembourg (July 14), and asked him to give Joan up to the Inquisition, to be tried by the laws of the Inquisition for the crimes of witchcraft, idolatry, and wrong doctrines about religion.

The Inquisitor was the head of a kind of religious Court, which tried people for not holding the right belief, or for witchcraft, or other religious offences. The rules of the Court, and the way of managing the trials, were what we think very unfair. But they were not more unfair than the methods used in Scotland after the Reformation. With us old women were tortured till they confessed that they were witches, and then were burned alive, sometimes seven or eight of them at once, for crimes which nobody could possibly commit.

That went on in Scotland till the country was united to England, at the beginning of the eighteenth century, and the laws against witchcraft were not abolished till 1736. Many of the Presbyterian ministers, who were active in hunting for witches and having them put to horrid tortures, were very angry that the witchcraft laws were abolished. The Inquisition was better than the ministers and magistrates in one way: if a witch confessed, and promised not to do it again, she was not put to death, but kept in prison. In Scotland the people accused of witchcraft had not even this chance, which did not help Joan, as we shall see.

All this is told here, to show that the French were not more stupid and cruel four hundred years ago, than we were in Scotland, two hundred years ago. But it was a fearful thing to fall into the hands of the Inquisition, and therefore the French King and his subjects should have paid Joan's ransom at once or rescued her by force of arms. But not a coin was paid, and not a sword was drawn to ransom or to rescue her. The people who advised the King had never liked her, and now the King left her to her fate. She could have taken a bitter revenge on him, if she had chosen to tell tales; but she was loyal to the last, like Montrose to Charles II.

Of course Joan was not a witch, and was a most religious girl, but she did not deny that she had talked with spirits, the spirits of the Saints; and her judges, who hated her, could say, and did say, that these spirits were devils, in disguise, and that therefore she was a witch. She always had known that they would do this, if they got the chance.

Jean de Luxembourg did not hand Joan over to the priests at once: probably he was waiting to see if he could not get a better price from her French friends than from her English enemies. The Bishop of Beauvais was Joan's worst enemy: his odious name was Pierre Cauchon, and in July he kept pressing the Duke of Burgundy, then still besieging Compiègne, to make Jean give up the Maid. Jean kept the Maid in a castle called Beaulieu till August, and then sent her to another castle, Beaurevoir, near Cambrai, far to the north, where it would be more difficult for her friends like Dunois and d'Alencon to come and rescue her by force, which we do not hear that they ever tried to do, though perhaps they did. The brave Xaintrailles was doing a thing that Joan longed for even more than for her freedom. She was taken in fighting to help the town of Compiègne, of which she was very fond, and her great grief at Beaulieu and Beaurevoir was that Compiègne was likely to be taken by the Burgundians and English, who threatened to put the people to death. All this while Xaintrailles was preparing a small army to deliver Compiègne.

At Beaurevoir the ladies of the castle were kinsfolk of Jean de Luxembourg. They were good women, and very kind to Joan, and they knelt to Jean, weeping, and asking him to give her back to her friends. But he wanted his money, like the men who sold Sir William Wallace to the English, and the great Montrose to the preachers and Parliament.

So Jean sold the Maid to the English. Joan knew this, and knew what she had to expect. She was allowed to take the air on the flat roof of the great tower at Leaurevoir, which was 60 feet high. She was not thinking so much of herself as of Compiègne. If she could escape she would try to make her way to Compiègne, and help the people to fight for their liberty and their lives. But how could she escape? She hoped that, if she leaped from the top of the tower, her Saints would bear her up in their arms, and not let her be hurt by the fall. So she asked them if she might leap down, but St. Catherine said, No; she

must not leap. God would help her and the people of Compiègne.
But Jean would not listen, this time, to the Voice. She said that, if the leap was wrong, she would rather trust her soul to the mercy of God, than her body to the English. And she must go to Compiègne, for she heard that, when the town was taken, all the people, old and young, were to be put to the sword.

Then she leaped, and there she lay. She was not hurt, not a bone of her was broken, which is an extraordinary thing, but she could not move a limb. The people of the castle came and took her back to her prison room. She did not know what had happened, and for three days she ate nothing. Then her memory came back to her and to her sorrows. Why was she not allowed to die! St. Catherine told her that she had sinned, and must confess, and ask the Divine mercy. But she was to go through with her appointed task. "Take no care for thy torment," said the Voice; "thence shalt thou come into Paradise." Moreover, St. Catherine promised that Compiègne should be rescued before Martinmas. That was the last good news, and the last happy thing that came to Joan in the days of her life; for, just before Martinmas, her friend, Pothon de Xaintrailles, rode with his men-at-arms through the forest of Compiègne, whilst others of the French attacked the English and Burgundians on the farther side of the Oise, and so the Saint kept her promise, and Compiègne was saved.

CHAPTER XVI. THE TRIAL OF THE MAID

AS Joan was a woman, and a prisoner of the Church, when the English had handed her over to the priests, she ought to have been kept in gentle prison, and with only women about her. But the English were very cruel. They had a kind of cage made, called a huche, and put in a strong room in the Castle of Rouen. In this cage they kept Joan, with chains on her legs, which were fastened to a strong post or beam of the bed. Five common soldiers kept watch in the room, day and night; the eyes of men were always on the most modest of girls. We see how much they feared her. They wished to have her proved a witch, and one who dealt with devils, to take away the shame of having been defeated by a girl, and also to disgrace the French King by making the world believe that he had been helped by a sorceress and her evil spirits. In truth, if you read Henry VI., Part L, by Shakespeare, you will see just what the English thought about the Maid. Shakespeare, of course, did not know the true story of Joan, and he makes her say abominable things, which not even her enemies brought up against her at her Trial. If Shakespeare wrote the play, he did not care a penny for the truth of the story. He sends Joan to Bordeaux, where she never was in her life, and makes "Fiends" (that is, her Saints) appear to her, and show that they will help her no longer. So she offers her very soul as a sacrifice for the sake of France:

"Then take my soul, my body, soul and all,
Before that England give the French the foil."

Later she turns on the English, and says what she might have said with truth:

"I never had to do with wicked spirits:
But you, that are polluted with your lusts,
Stained with the guiltless blood of innocents,
Corrupt and tainted with a thousand vices,
Because you want the grace that others have,
You judge it straight a thing impossible
To compass wonders but by help of devils."

The English had devils on their own side, the cruel priests and Bishop Cauchon, whom they had promised to make Archbishop of Rouen. But he never got it.
For three months these people examined Joan every day, sometimes all shouting at her at once, so that she said, "Gentlemen, if you please, one at a time." She had no advocate, who knew the law, to help her to defend herself. But once, when she appealed to the Council of Basle, a Council cf the Church which was then sitting, they bade her be silent, and told the clerk who took down everything in writing, in French, not to write down her appeal. There is nothing about this in the Latin

book of the Trial, translated from the French, but in the French copy, mode in court, you see the place where the clerk's pen has stopped at the words, "and she appeals" (Et requiert, in French). He was going to write the rest. Now she had a right to appeal, and as the clergy at the Council of Basle were of many countries, they would not have taken the English side, but pronounced Joan innocent. The Bishops and clergy of the loyal French party at Poitiers, before she went to the war, had declared her innocent and a thing of God, after a long examination of her life up till April 1429. Joan often asked her judges to send for "the Poitiers book," where they would find answers to their questions about her early days; but they vexed her about everything, even about the fairy tree, on which the children used to hang their garlands. Their notion seems to have been that the fairies were her helpers, not the Saints, and that the fairies were evil spirits.

Joan had shown that, in war and politics, she was wiser than the soldiers and statesmen. She went straight at the work to be done —to beat the English, and to keep attacking them before they got back their confidence. At her Trial she showed that she was far wiser than the learned priests. They tried to prove that she was helped by fairies. She said that she did not believe there were any fairies: and though I would not say that there are none, there certainly are not so many, or so busy and powerful, as the priests supposed. They kept asking her about the prophecies of Merlin the Wizard: she thought nothing of Merlin the Wizard.

She vowed to speak truth in answer to questions, but she would not answer questions about her Saints and Voices, except when they gave her permission. The judges troubled her most about the secret of the King, and what she told him about that, before she went to the wars. You remember that the King had secretly prayed to know whether he really was the son of the late King or not, and that Joan told him of his prayer, and told him that he was the son of the late King, and had the right to be King himself. But she would tell the Judges nothing about all this matter. If she had, the English would have cried everywhere, "You see he is not certain himself that he is what he pretends to be. Our King of England is the only King of France."

Joan would not betray her King's doubts. She never would tell what happened. At last she cold a simple parable: an Angel came with a rich crown for the King. But, later, she explained that by the Angel she meant herself, and that by the Crown, she meant her having him crowned at Rheims. They never could get the King's secret out of her. At last they said they would put her to the torture. They took her to a horrible vault, full of abominable instruments for pinching, and tearing, and roasting, and screwing the bodies of men. There stood the executioner, with his arms bare, and his fire lit, and all his pincers, and ropes, and pulleys ready.
"Now will you tell us?" they said. Brave men had turned faint with terror in that vault, and had said anything that they were asked to say, rather than face the pain. There was a Marshal of France, Gilles de Rais, a nobleman who fought beside Joan at Orleans, at Les Tourelles, at Jargeau, at Pathay, and at Paris, and who carried the sacred vessel which the Angel brought, long ago, with holy oil, at the King's coronation. Later this man was accused by the Inquisition of the most horrible crimes. Among other things, he was said to have sacrificed children to the devil, and to have killed hundreds of little boys for his own amusement. But hundreds of little boys were not proved to be missing, and none of their remains were ever found. Gilles de

Rais denied these horrible charges; he said he was innocent, and, for all that we know, he was. But they took him to the torture vault, and showed him the engines of torment, and he confessed everything, so that he might be put to death without torture, which was done.

Joan did not fear and turn faint. She said, "Torture me if you please. Tear my body to pieces. Whatever I say in my pains will not be true, and as soon as I am released I will deny that it was true. Now, go on!" Many priests wished to go on, but more, even of these cruel enemies, said, "No!" they would not torture the girl.

"What a brave lass. Pity she is not English!" one of the English lords said, when he saw Joan standing up against the crowd of priests and lawyers.

Remember that, for six weeks, during Lent, Joan took no food all day. There she stood, starving, and answering everybody, always bravely, always courteously, always wisely, and sometimes even merrily. They kept asking her the same questions on different days, to try to make her vary in her answers. All the answers were written down. Once they said she had answered differently before, and, when the book was examined, it proved that there was some mistake in the thing, and that Jean was in the right. She was much pleased, and said to the clerk, "If you make mistakes again, I will pull your ears."

They troubled her very much about wearing boy's dress. She said that, when among men in war, it was better and more proper. She was still among men, with soldiers in her room, day and night, which was quite unlawful; she should have had only women about her. She would not put on women's dress while she was among men, and was quite in the right.

She could hear her Voices in Court, but not clearly on account of the noise. Once, I suppose, she heard them, for she suddenly said, in the middle of an answer to a question about the letters which were written for her when she was in the wars:

"Before seven years are passed the English will lose a greater stake than they have lost at Orleans; they will lose everything in France."

Before the seven years were out they lost Paris, a much greater stake than Orleans, as Paris was the chief town and the largest They went on losing till they lost everything in France, even all that they had held for hundreds of years.

The Judges insisted that she should submit to the Church. Joan asked nothing better. "Take me to the Pope, and I will answer him, for I know and believe that we should obey our Holy Father, the Pope, who is in Rome." Or she would answer the Council of the whole Church at Basle, but, as I said, the Bishop Cauchon stopped the clerk when he was writing down the words. The Judges said "We are the Church; answer us and obey us." But, of course, they were not the Church; they were only a set of disloyal French priests who sided against their own country, and helped the English.

CHAPTER XVII. HOW THE PRIESTS BETRAYED THE MAID

AT last, on May 24, 1431, they determined to force her to acknowledge herself in the wrong, and to deny her Saints. On that day they took her to the graveyard of the Church of St. Ouen. Two platforms had been built; on one stood the wretched Cauchon with his gang; Joan was placed on the other. There was also a stake with faggots, for burning Joan. They had ready two written papers: on one it was written that Joan would submit to them, and wear woman's dress. On the other was a long statement that her Saints were evil spirits, and that she had done all sorts of wrong things. She was told that if she would sign the short paper, and wear womans dress, she would be put in gentle prison, with women about her instead of English soldiers. Seeing the fire ready, Jean repeated the short form of words, and made her mark, smiling, on the piece of paper that they gave her, but it was the paper with the long speech, accusing herself of crimes and denying her Saints.
This is what we are told, but, later, she showed that she thought she had denied her Saints, so it is not easy to be quite sure of what happened. It is certain that Cauchon broke his word. She was not taken away from her cruel prison and the English

soldiers, as was promised. She was given woman's dress; but, as they were determined to make her "relapse," that is, return to the sin of wearing man's dress, for then they could burn her, they put her boy's dress in her room, and so acted that she was obliged to put it on. It is a horrid story, not fit to be told, of cruelty and falseness.

"Now we have her!" said Cauchon to an Englishman.

They went to her, and asked her if the Voices had come to her again?

"Yes!"

"What did they say?"

"St. Catherine and St. Margaret told me that I had done very wrong, when I said what I did to save my life, and that I was damning myself to save my life."

"Then you believe that the Voices were the voices of the Saints."

"Yes, I believe that, and that the Voices come from God;" and she said that she did not mean ever to have denied it.

On the day of her burning, the Bishop and the rest went to Joan again, and wrote out a statement that she left it to the Church to say whether her Voices were good or bad. The Church has decided that they were good, and has given Joan the title of "Venerable," which is the first step toward proclaiming her to be one of the Saints. Whatever the Voices were, she said they were real, not fancied things.

But this paper does not count, for the clerk who took all the notes refused to go with the Bishop to see Joan, that time, saying that it was no part of the law, and that they went as private men, not as Judges, and he had the courage not to sign the paper. He was an honest man, and thought Joan a good girl, unlawfully treated, and was very sorry for her. "He never wept so much for any sorrow in all his life, and for a month he could not be quiet for sorrow: and he bought a book of prayers and

prayed for the soul of the Maid."
This honest man's name was Gilbert Manchon.

CHAPTER XVIII. THE END OF THE MAID

THEY burned her cruelly to death in the market-place of Rouen, with eight hundred soldiers round the stake, lest any should attempt to save her. They had put a false accusation on a paper cap, and set it on her head: it was written that she was "Heretic, Relapsed, Apostate, Idolatress." This was her reward for the bravest and best life that was ever lived.
She came to her own and her own received her not.
There was with her a priest who pitied her, not one of her Judges—Brother Isambert de la Pierre, of the order of St. Augustine. Joan asked him to bring her a cross, and to hold it up before her eyes while she was burning. "Saith moreover that while she was in the fire she ceased never to call loudly on the Holy Name of Jesus; always, too, imploring: ceaselessly the help of the Saints in Paradise; and more, when the end was now come, she bowed her head, and gave up her spirit, calling on the name of Jesus."
The Saints had said to her, long before: "Bear your torment lightly: thence shall you come into the kingdom of Paradise."
So died Joan the Maid.
It is said by some who were present, that even the English Cardinal, Beaufort, wept when he saw the Maid die: "crocodiles' tears!" One of the secretaries of Henry VI. (who himself was

only a little boy) said, "We are all lost. We have burned a Saint!" They were all lost. The curse of their cruelty did not depart from them. Driven by the French and Scots from province to province, and from town to town, the English returned home, tore and rent each other; murdering their princes and nobles on the scaffold, and slaying them as prisoners of war on the field; and stabbing and smothering them in chambers of the Tower; York and Lancaster devouring each other; the man Henry VI. was driven from home to wander by the waves at St. Andrews, before he wandered back to England and the dagger stroke-these things were the reward the English won, after they had burned a Saint, they ate the bread and drank the cup of their own greed and cruelty all through the Wars of the Roses. They brought shame upon their name which Time can never wash away; they did the Devil's work, and took the Devil's wages. Soon Henry VIII. was butchering his wives and burning Catholics and Protestants, now one, now the other, as the humour seized him.

Joan had said to the Archbishop, at Rheims, that she knew not where she would die, or where she would be buried. Her ashes were never laid in the earth; she had no grave. The English, that men might forget her, threw her ashes into the sea. There remains no relic of Joan of Arc; no portrait, nothing she ever wore, no cup or sword or jewel that she ever touched. But she is not forgotten; she never will be forgotten. On every Eighth of May, the day when she turned the tide of English conquest, a procession in her honour goes through the streets of Orleans, the city that she saved; and though the Protestants, at the Reformation, destroyed her statue that knelt before the Fair Cross on the bridge, she has statues in many of the towns in France. She was driven from the gate of Paris, but near the place where she lay wounded in the ditch, is her statue, showing her on horseback, in armour.

CHAPTER XIX. THE SECOND TRIAL OF THE MAID

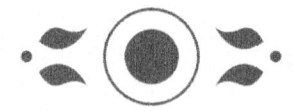

THE rich and the strong had not paid a franc, or drawn a sword to ransom or to rescue Joan. The poor had prayed for her, and the written prayers which they used may still be seen. Probably the others would have been glad to let Joan's memory perish, but to do this was not convenient. If Joan had been a witch, a heretic, an impostor, an apostate, as was declared in her condemnation, then the King had won his battles by the help of a heretic and a witch. Twenty years after Joan's martyrdom, when the King had recovered Normandy and Rouen, he thought it time to take care of his own character, and to inquire into the charges on which she was found guilty. It is fair to say that he could not do this properly till he was master of Rouen, the place at which she was tried. Some of the people concerned were asked questions, such as the good clerk, Manchon, and Deaupèrc, one of the Judges. He was a man of some sense: he did not think that Joan was a witch, but that she was a fanciful girl, who thought that she saw Saints and heard Voices, when she neither saw nor heard anything. Many mad people hear Voices which are also mad; Joan's Voices were perfectly sane and wise, and told her things that she could not have known of herself.

Not much came of this examination, but, two years later, Joan's mother and brothers prayed for a new trial to clear the character of the family. It is the most extraordinary thing that, up to this year, 1452, Joan's brothers and cousins seem to have been living, on the best terms, with the woman who pretended to be Joan, and said that she had not been burned, but had escaped. This was a jolly kind of woman, fond of eating and drinking and playing tennis.

Why Joan's brothers and cousins continued to be friendly with her after the King found her out, because she did not know his secret, is the greatest of puzzles, for she was a detected impostor, and no money could be got from the connection with her. Another very amazing thing is that, in 1436, an aunt of the Duke of Burgundy, Madame de Luxembourg, entertained the impostor, while the whole town of Orleans welcomed her, and made her presents, and ceased holding a religious service on the day of Joan's death, for here, they said, she was, quite well and merry! Moreover the town's books of accounts, at Orleans, show that they paid a pension to Joan's mother as "Mother of the Maid," till 1452, when they say "Mother of the late Maid." For now, as Joan's family were trying to have her character cleared, they admitted that she was dead, burned to death in 1431, as, of course, she really was. There are not many things more curious than this story of the False Maid.

However, at last Joan's family gave up the impostor, and, five years later, she was imprisoned, and let out again, and that is the last we hear of her. The new Trial lingered on, was begun, and put off, and begun again in 1455. Cauchon was dead by this time; nothing could be done to him. Scores of witnesses came and told the stories given at the beginning of this book, showing how Joan was the best and most religious of girls, and very kind to people even more poor than herself, and very industrious in knitting and sewing and helping her mother. Every one who was still alive, that had known her in the wars, came, like d'Alençon, and Dunois, and d'Aulon, and her confessor: and many others came, and told about Joan in the wars, how brave she was and modest, and the stories of what she had suffered in prison, and about the unfairness of her trial, were repeated.

The end was that the Court of Inquiry-declared her trial to have been full of unlawfulness and cruelty, and they abolished the sentence against her and took off all the shameful reproaches, and ordered a beautiful cross to be erected to her memory in the place where she was burned to death.

So here ends the story of the Life and Death of Joan the Maid.

CPSIA information can be obtained
at www.ICGtesting.com
Printed in the USA
LVOW04s1109091215
466111LV00015B/159/P